SPOTLIGHT ON NATIVE AMERICANS

SHAWNEE

Kadeem Jones

PowerKiDS
press™

New York

Published in 2016 by The Rosen Publishing Group, Inc.
29 East 21st Street, New York, NY 10010

First Edition

Book Design: Samantha DeMartin
Material reviewed by: Donald A. Grinde, Jr., Professor of Transnational/American Studies at the State University of New York at Buffalo.

Library of Congress Cataloging-in-Publication Data

Jones, Kadeem, author.
  Shawnee / Kadeem Jones.
     pages cm. — (Spotlight on Native Americans)
  Includes index.
  ISBN 978-1-5081-4124-2 (pbk.)
  ISBN 978-1-5081-4125-9 (6 pack)
  ISBN 978-1-5081-4127-3 (library binding)
  1. Shawnee Indians—Juvenile literature. I. Title.
  E99.S35J65 2016
  974.004'97317—dc23
                        2015034688

Manufactured in the United States of America

CPSIA Compliance Information: Batch #BW16PK: For Further Information contact Rosen Publishing, New York, New York at 1-800-237-9932

CONTENTS

SHAWNEE ORIGINS. 4

ANCESTORS OF THE SHAWNEES 6

FIRST ENCOUNTERS. 8

LIFE AFTER THE REVOLUTION 10

LOSING LAND, SPLITTING UP 12

HOW THEY LIVED 14

TRADITIONAL SHAWNEE BELIEFS. 18

LOSING POWER AND GAINING IT BACK 22

DIFFERENT BANDS 24

TODAY'S SHAWNEES. 26

THE FUTURE OF THE SHAWNEE. 28

GLOSSARY 30

FOR MORE INFORMATION 31

INDEX 32

SHAWNEE ORIGINS
CHAPTER 1

The Shawnees once lived as far north as today's New York and as far south as Georgia. This Algonquian-speaking people moved around the area, bringing their rich **culture** with them and adopting many **traditions** from other native peoples. Today, the **descendants** of those people mostly live in Oklahoma. In this book, you'll learn about the Shawnee people—their history, their culture, and how they live today.

Shawnee

EASTERN WOODLANDS REGION

Where did the Shawnees come from? Many people believe the ancestors of all native peoples in the Americas came from Asia around 12,000 years ago. During this time, there was an **ice age**, which caused sea levels to go down.

The Shawnees eventually settled in the eastern part of North America in an area known as the Eastern Woodlands.

When this happened, a land bridge between Asia and the Americas appeared, allowing people to cross over.

These people eventually spread throughout North and South America and created their own cultures based on their environment, or surroundings. At first, they moved around in search of animals to hunt. In time, individual groups, including the Shawnees, began to farm during part of the year, which helped them create permanent homes and villages.

Shawnee powwow

ANCESTORS OF THE SHAWNEES

CHAPTER 2

The ancestors of the Shawnees were the Mound Builders. These people built earthen mounds throughout eastern and midwestern North America—from the Great Lakes to the Gulf of Mexico. The Mound Builders existed for about 5,000 years. This stretch of time is broken into three major periods: Archaic, Woodland, and Mississippian.

It's believed the Shawnees descended from the Adena and Hopewell peoples—two groups that lived during the Woodland Period. The Adena existed from around 1000 BC to AD 100, while the Hopewell lived from around 100 BC to around AD 500. They settled along rivers in the midwestern and

Great Serpent Mound

northeastern parts of North America, especially in today's Ohio River valley. Other descendants of these peoples include the Cherokee, Seminole, Osage, Fox, and Creek peoples.

The dome-shaped mounds built by these people were made of dirt and usually were used for burial. Mound Builders left goods such as pottery inside the mounds. The Adena Mound in Chillicothe, Ohio, was **excavated** around 1901. In it, an **archaeologist** named William C. Mills found a decorative pipe, known as the Adena Effigy Pipe. Other mounds were used for ceremonies and took on different shapes, such as the Great Serpent Mound near Hillsboro, Ohio.

This Adena mound has been preserved throughout the years. Each mound holds clues to the history of the Shawnees' ancestors.

Adena Mound

FIRST ENCOUNTERS
CHAPTER 3

For thousands of years, the Shawnees traded goods and shared **customs** with other native peoples. They were known as brave warriors. They built a successful community that lived by hunting, gathering, and farming.

In 1677, the Shawnee first encountered French traders. In the coming years, encounters with white settlers became more frequent. The Shawnees began a trading relationship with the French. When the French and British went to war, the Shawnees initially fought on the French side. This war, called the French and Indian War, lasted from 1754 to 1763.

As more white settlers came to North America, they brought deadly illnesses, guns, and a hunger for land. At first, many paid the native peoples for land or made deals. Eventually, the settlers began taking native land without permission. This led to a series of bloody battles. In 1774, the Virginia militia, or military, attacked the Shawnees for their land in Kentucky. This started Lord Dunmore's War. On October 10, 1774, the Shawnees were defeated at the Battle of Point Pleasant and lost their hunting grounds to white settlers.

In 1758, in the middle of the French and Indian War, the Shawnees switched to the British side. In exchange for peace, the Shawnees and other native peoples were promised their hunting grounds west of the Allegheny Mountains after the war.

LIFE AFTER THE REVOLUTION

CHAPTER 4

From 1775 to 1783, many Shawnees fought alongside the British in the American Revolution. However, some Shawnees didn't want to be involved in the American Revolution. They sought peace by leaving Ohio for Spanish Louisiana, before settling near today's Cape Girardeau, Missouri. Some of them left for today's Texas, Louisiana, and Alabama, where they lived in scattered groups. In 1825, these Shawnees accepted a **reservation** in Kansas. Some stayed there, while many of the scattered groups eventually went to Indian Territory in Oklahoma. Those who left for Indian Territory became known as the Absentee Shawnees.

After the revolution, white settlement spread even further, and many native peoples lost their land. The Shawnees partnered with the Delaware, Miami, Wyandot, and Mingo peoples, among others. This partnership, called the Western Confederacy, aimed to make the Ohio River the boundary between the United States and native lands.

That would include removing settlers from Kentucky and Ohio. Violence broke out between U.S. citizens and native peoples in a series of battles between 1785 and 1795, which became known as the Northwest Indian War. The native peoples lost the war and had to sign the Treaty of Greenville, which gave even more land in Ohio to the United States.

Shawnee chief Blue Jacket led Native American forces against the U.S. Army at the Battle of Fallen Timbers, shown here, in 1794.

LOSING LAND, SPLITTING UP

CHAPTER 5

The Northwest Indian War gave rise to a Shawnee warrior named Tecumseh, one of the greatest leaders of the Shawnee. He formed another Indian confederation to fight against the white settlers. He assembled a huge force of native people to fight against U.S. forces alongside the British during the War of 1812. Tecumseh also believed words could be as powerful as fighting. He became a spokesman for native peoples. When Tecumseh died in 1813, it marked an end to Shawnee resistance.

In 1817, Shawnees signed the Treaty of Fort Meigs. This treaty set up three reservations in Ohio: Lewistown, Hog Creek, and Wapakoneta. In 1830, the Indian Removal Act went into effect. Its goal was to move all native peoples west of

Tecumseh

the Mississippi River. Like many others, the Shawnees had to leave their homes again and make long journeys on foot. Yet another treaty forced the Shawnees living on the Wapakoneta and Hog Creek Reservations to leave for a new reservation in Kansas. The Shawnees living on the Lewistown Reservation, however, moved directly to Indian Territory in Oklahoma.

Kansas Shawnees faced injustice and violence, and they were eventually forced to move to northeastern Oklahoma to live with the Cherokee Nation. In 1869, these Shawnees became citizens of the Cherokee Nation and were given their own land to create their own communities.

Tenskwatawa

Tecumseh brought many nations together to try to stop white settlers from stealing land from native peoples. Tecumseh's brother, Tenskwatawa, was known as the Prophet. He believed he was told by a higher being that Shawnees should go back to traditional ways of life.

HOW THEY LIVED
CHAPTER 6

Though the Shawnees lost their homelands and had to separate, they're united by a common history and traditions. How did the Shawnees live in the past?

The Shawnee people lived in villages that had their own government. They were ruled by a principal chief who was elected by other Shawnee leaders. If the people didn't like the chief, he could be replaced. Each village also had a tribal council, which made many important decisions for the community. War chiefs led the Shawnees in their battles, and they were chosen for their talents and courage.

Shawnee villages each had a council house, which was large and made of wood. Families lived in wigwams, which were round houses that could be taken apart in case the people had to move. Wigwams were made out of tree bark, cattails, thick grass, and other materials found in nature. Shawnees usually lived in villages in summer and moved around in smaller groups in search of food in winter.

The Shawnees were hunters, but they also farmed. Shawnee men were in charge of hunting and fishing.

Women stayed home to cook, farm, and take care of the children. They played a very important part in agriculture, which gave them a lot of power in the community. They were also responsible for establishing kinship and support within their clan.

Shawnees used wood for many things, including making their wigwams, crafting bows and arrows for hunting, and building canoes to travel by water.

The Shawnees dressed like many of the Eastern Woodland peoples. Women wore skirts, while men wore breechcloths. Breechcloths were pieces of clothing worn around the hips. People dressed for the weather. When it was cold, men and women wore leggings and coats. They often went barefoot, but they sometimes wore moccasins, or soft shoes, on their feet. Since the Shawnees traded with many other peoples, they sometimes took on other styles of dress. When white settlers arrived, Shawnees started wearing European-style clothing.

Traditional Shawnees usually grew their hair long. Warriors sometimes shaved the sides of their head and left a strip of hair down the middle. Sometimes Shawnees wore a beaded headband, and feathers were worn for important events and ceremonies.

The Shawnees were skilled at using beads to make jewelry and belts. They created special beads, called wampum, from sea shells. Wampum beads were used to make decorative belts with many images and patterns. Sometimes the belts had a special meaning, such as a family story. Wampum beads were so important to the Shawnees and other neighboring tribes that they were used as **currency**.

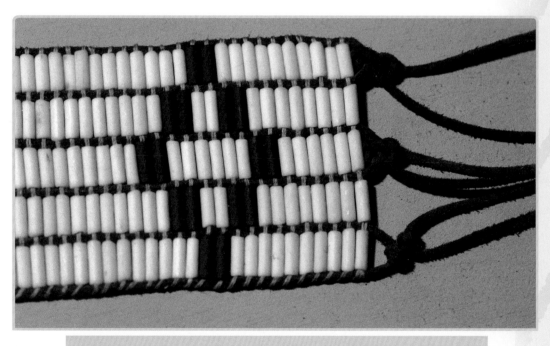

This is a traditional Shawnee wampum belt. The wampum beads are held together with leather string.

TRADITIONAL SHAWNEE BELIEFS

CHAPTER 7

Like most native peoples, the Shawnees' beliefs were heavily influenced by their environment. Many stories and figures in their spiritual life had to do with nature. The Shawnees believed that a supreme being named Mishe Moneto decided to create the earth and sent Kokumthena to do it.

Kokumthena is an important spiritual figure for the Shawnees. Her name means "our grandmother," and she is an old woman who created the earth and will someday end it. Kokumthena speaks a language only young children can understand. Some believe Kokumthena is weaving a blanket, and when she finishes that blanket, she will save the good people and destroy the bad people. The figure of Kokumthena shows the importance of women, especially elderly women, within the Shawnee society.

The Shawnees believe in many spiritual figures that present themselves in nature, too. They believe in Cyclone

Person, or a spirit that causes storms. Some say the dark swirls of a tornado are Cyclone Person's long hair. The Shawnees also believe in a giant bird whose wings cause thunder when it flies. Some stories tell of a horned serpent that lives underwater, waiting to eat people.

The Shawnees held big dances in celebration of the changing seasons. It was their way of giving thanks to Mishe Moneto and Kokumthena. Today, many traditional dances are still practiced.

The Shawnees have long told a story about how they came to be. This is called their origin story. The Shawnees' origin story has many things in common with other Algonquian creation stories.

There are many variations of the Shawnee origin story. The most common story says that the Shawnees came from a different world. Their world was an island on the back of a huge turtle. They longed to leave the island, but couldn't go anywhere because there was water on all sides. The turtle began moving, and it brought them to this world, where they made their home.

Kokumthena is also an important part of Shawnee creation stories because they believe she created the earth. Many people believe Kokumthena warned the Shawnees of a great white spirit who would try to destroy them. Others believe she warned of a giant snake that would come out of the sea to harm the Shawnees. When Europeans arrived, the Shawnees saw it as a sign that the serpent or white spirit had arrived.

This piece of artwork illustrates the Iroquois creation story, which is very similar to the Shawnee creation story. Both tell of a huge turtle that brought them to their homeland.

LOSING POWER AND GAINING IT BACK

CHAPTER 8

In 1907, Oklahoma became a state. That meant all native peoples living in Indian Territory had to become citizens of the United States. White settlers, called homesteaders, rushed to the area to claim land, which they often stole from the native peoples. Reservations grew smaller, and injustices against native people worsened. Americans tried to break the native peoples, including the Shawnees, of their culture. They tried to force native children to adopt more "white" ways by sending them to boarding schools and stripping them of their heritage.

Fortunately, in the late 1960s, the American Indian Movement (AIM) began. Its goal was to regain culture and power for the native peoples living in the United States. AIM wanted native tribes to be recognized as **sovereign** nations, which means they'd rule themselves. Because of AIM, Native Americans who lived on reservations were given the right to reject certain U.S. laws and state taxes. This meant they could open casinos, or places for gambling, on reservations.

In the 1980s, the Shawnee Tribe, which had joined the Cherokee Nation, sought to become its own sovereign nation, separate from the Cherokees. Their request wasn't fully recognized until 2000, when Congress granted them sovereignty.

The American Indian Movement fought for the civil rights of all native peoples. Native Americans fought for sovereignty as well as their right to education, culture, and fair treatment. Today, one of the concerns of AIM and other Native American groups is the use of names such as Redskins for sports mascots, which this group is shown protesting.

DIFFERENT BANDS

CHAPTER 9

As the Shawnees were forced to move around, they began to split into different groups. These groups settled in new areas and began to create their own identity. For that reason, there are three federally recognized Shawnee groups: the Absentee Shawnee Tribe of Indians of Oklahoma, the Eastern Shawnee Tribe of Oklahoma, and the Shawnee Tribe, which used to be part of the Cherokee Nation. There are also smaller divisions of Shawnees that have banded together in common areas.

Each major Shawnee tribe has its own tribal government, identity, and way of life. However, they still hold a common history. How did each tribe form? The Absentee Shawnee Tribe first moved to Cape Girardeau, Missouri, then moved farther south, before moving to southern Oklahoma.

The Eastern Shawnee Tribe of Oklahoma came from the Lewistown Reservation, one of the three reservations created in northwest Ohio in 1817. They moved directly to

Indian Territory along with a group of Senecas, eventually becoming the Eastern Shawnee Tribe.

The Shawnee Tribe are the descendants of the Shawnees from Kansas that had to live with the Cherokee Nation in northeastern Oklahoma. Today, they are their own federally recognized tribe.

Each of the federally recognized Shawnee tribes has its own flag.

TODAY'S SHAWNEES
CHAPTER 10

Today's Shawnees try to keep their traditional ways of life alive even as they live in the modern world. They live in apartments and houses instead of wigwams. Many live on trust lands, which they often call reservations, even though there are differences between the two.

Each band of Shawnees has its own services, laws, businesses, governments, and traditions. Businesses include casinos, gift shops, stores, and car repair shops. The Absentee Shawnee Tribe has a governor to make **executive** decisions, while the Eastern Shawnee Tribe has a chief, and the Shawnee Tribe has a tribal administrator. Each tribe has its own court that upholds the laws of its government. The tribes offer educational services, social services, health programs, and help finding jobs. They keep their cultures alive by teaching their people about traditional dances, language basics, clothing, and **powwows**.

Exceptional modern Shawnees include guitarist Link Wray and author Nas'Naga. Link Wray was half-Shawnee, and he became an influential figure in the beginnings of rock and roll. Nas'Naga was the pen name of a Shawnee writer, artist, and poet named Roger W. Russell. He wrote the young adult novel *Indians' Summer*, which was published in 1975.

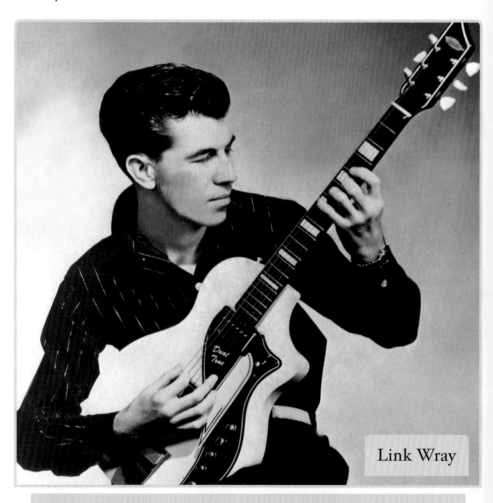

Link Wray

Born in 1929, Link Wray was a songwriter, guitarist, and singer. He rose to fame in the 1950s with songs such as "Rumble" and "Rawhide." He performed a song called "Shawnee" and often spoke of his heritage.

THE FUTURE OF THE SHAWNEE

CHAPTER 11

The Shawnee people have come a long way from their ancestral homelands. Faced with injustice, they traveled long distances to finally settle in Oklahoma. They faced **poverty**, unfair treatment, and loss of land. Unfortunately, today's Shawnees still face many challenges, such as poverty, health problems, and poor living conditions.

The future of the Shawnees is sure to improve with each generation, thanks to advancements in community services and education. They're working harder than ever to rebuild their culture and keep it alive. Shawnee artists still create traditional clothing, beaded jewelry, and blankets. Artists, such as Ruthe Blalock Jones, make paintings that represent the history and culture of the Shawnee people. The Absentee Shawnee Tribe Library and Archives houses many important Shawnee **artifacts**, as well as over 700 books and 300 documents that are important to their culture. The Eastern Shawnee Tribe holds a three-day powwow every year that includes traditional dancing, foods, and art.

Today's Shawnees are working to preserve their language, art, dances, and stories for generations to come.

This Shawnee man attends the Gathering of Nations powwow dressed in a feather hat and face paint.

GLOSSARY

archaeologist: Someone who studies the bones, tools, and other objects left behind by ancient people.

artifact: An object remaining from a past period.

culture: The arts, beliefs, and customs that form a people's way of life.

currency: Something used as payment for something else.

custom: An action or way of behaving that's usual and traditional among people in a certain group.

descendant: A relative of someone who lived in an earlier time.

excavate: To uncover something by removing the earth surrounding it.

executive: Having to do with the carrying out of a law.

ice age: A period during which temperatures fall worldwide and large areas are covered with glaciers.

poverty: The state of being poor.

powwow: A social gathering of Native Americans that usually includes dancing.

reservation: Land set aside by the government for a specific Native American group or groups to live on.

sovereign: Having independent authority and the right to govern itself.

tradition: A way of thinking, behaving, or doing something that's been used by people in a particular society for a long time.

FOR MORE INFORMATION

BOOKS

Gibson, Karen Bush. *Native American History for Kids: With 21 Activities*. Chicago, IL: Chicago Review Press, 2010.

Tieck, Sarah. *Shawnee*. Edina, Minnesota: ABDO Publishing, 2015.

Zimmerman, Dwight Jon. *Tecumseh: Shooting Star of the Shawnee*. New York, NY: Sterling Publishing, 2010.

WEBSITES

Due to the changing nature of Internet links, PowerKids Press has developed an online list of websites related to the subject of this book. This site is updated regularly. Please use this link to access the list: www.powerkidslinks.com/sona/shaw

INDEX

A

Absentee Shawnee Tribe of
    Indians, 24, 26, 28
American Indian Movement (AIM),
    22, 23

B

Blue Jacket, 11
breechcloths, 16

C

Cherokee Nation, 13, 23, 24, 25

E

Eastern Shawnee Tribe, 24, 25,
    26, 28
Eastern Woodlands, 4, 16

F

French and Indian War, 8, 9

G

Great Serpent Mound, 6, 7

H

Hog Creek Reservation, 12, 13

I

Indian Removal Act, 12
Indian Territory, 10, 13, 22, 25

K

Kansas, 10, 13, 25
Kentucky, 8, 11
Kokumthena, 18, 19, 20

L

Lewistown Reservation, 12, 13, 24
Lord Dunmore's War, 8

M

Mills, William C., 7
Mishe Moneto, 18, 19
Mississippian Period, 6
Mound Builders, 6, 7

N

Nas'Naga, 26
Northwest Indian War, 11, 12

O

Ohio, 7, 10, 11, 12, 24
Oklahoma, 4, 10, 13, 22, 24,
    25, 28
origin story, 20

R

Russell, Roger W., 27

S

Shawnee Tribe, 23, 24, 25, 26

T

Tecumseh, 12, 13
Tenskwatawa, 13
Treaty of Fort Meigs, 12
Treaty of Greenville, 11

W

wampum, 17
Wapakoneta Reservation, 12, 13
Western Confederacy, 10
wigwams, 14, 15, 26
Woodland Period, 6
Wray, Link, 26, 27